בִּרְכוֹת הַפְטָרָה

The Torah is the first part of the Bible (תַּנַ"ךְ); the Book of Prophets (נְבִיאִים) is the second; and Writings (כְּתוּבִים), which includes psalms, poems, and proverbs, is the third. At the conclusion of the Torah reading on Shabbat and on holidays, an honored person in the congregation reads a section from the Book of Prophets called the הַפְטָרָה ("conclusion"). The haftarah is often related by theme to that week's Torah portion or to a holiday season. When you become a Bar or Bat Mitzvah and are called up to the Torah for the first time, you will be the one to chant the haftarah that day!

Our tradition teaches that the prophets were learned, righteous people who spread the word of the Torah to the Jewish people. They were the conscience of the Jews. The truths taught by the prophets are told in the haftarah and help us to better understand important ideas or values found in the Torah.

We say a blessing before chanting the haftarah. Because the prophets were so important in communicating God's word, this blessing praises God for the fact that the Israelites had prophets.

BLESSING BEFORE THE HAFTARAH READING

Practice reading the blessing aloud.

1. בָּרוּךְ אַתָּה, יְיָ אֱלֹהֵינוּ, מֶלֶךְ הָעוֹלָם, אֲשֶׁר בָּחַר

2. בִּנְבִיאִים טוֹבִים, וְרָצָה בְדִבְרֵיהֶם הַנֶּאֱמָרִים בֶּאֱמֶת.

3. בָּרוּךְ אַתָּה יְיָ, הַבּוֹחֵר בַּתּוֹרָה, וּבְמשֶׁה עַבְדּוֹ,

4. וּבְיִשְׂרָאֵל עַמּוֹ, וּבִנְבִיאֵי הָאֱמֶת וָצֶדֶק.

Praised are You, Adonai our God, Ruler of the world, who chose
good (faithful) prophets, and was pleased with their words spoken in truth.
Praised are You, Adonai, the One who takes delight in (chooses) the Torah, and in Moses, God's
servant, and in Israel, God's people, and in prophets of truth and righteousness (justice).

בָּחַר

chose

(בְּ)נְבִיאִים

prophets

טוֹבִים

good (faithful)

הַנֶּאֱמָרִים

spoken

בֶּאֱמֶת

in truth

הַבּוֹחֵר

the one who chooses

עַבְדּוֹ

God's servant

עַמּוֹ

God's people

וְצֶדֶק

and righteousness (justice)

THE FAMILY CONNECTION

There are three sets of related words in the blessing before the הַפְטָרָה reading.

3	2	1
בֶּאֱמֶת	בִּנְבִיאִים	בָּחַר
הָאֱמֶת	וּבְנְבִיאֵי	הַבּוֹחֵר

Write the number of the related words next to their English meaning.

_____ prophets

_____ choose

_____ truth

It may seem as though you find the number 13 everywhere you look in the year you become a Bar or Bat Mitzvah.

MAKE ME A MATCH!

Connect the Hebrew word to its English meaning.

God's people   טוֹבִים

and righteousness (justice)   הַנֶּאֱמָרִים

good (faithful)   עַבְדּוֹ

spoken   עַמּוֹ

God's servant   וְצֶדֶק

אֲשֶׁר בָּחַר בִּנְבִיאִים טוֹבִים
"who chose good (faithful) prophets"

בָּחַר means "chose."

נְבִיאִים is the plural of נָבִיא.

Circle the part of נְבִיאִים that shows it is plural: נְבִיאִים

נָבִיא means _____.

נְבִיאִים means _____.

טוֹבִים is an adjective describing נְבִיאִים.

Circle the part of טוֹבִים that shows it is plural: טוֹבִים

טוֹב means _____.

טוֹבִים means _____.

הַנֶּאֱמָרִים בֶּאֱמֶת "spoken in truth"

הַנֶּאֱמָרִים means "spoken."

The root letters of הַנֶּאֱמָרִים are אמר.

אמר means "speak" or "say."

בֶּאֱמֶת means "in truth."

Read the following phrases aloud. Circle the words with the root אמר.

1. הָאֵל הַנֶּאֱמָן, הָאוֹמֵר וְעוֹשֶׂה
2. יִהְיוּ לְרָצוֹן אִמְרֵי פִי
3. חֲבֵרִים כָּל־יִשְׂרָאֵל, וְנֹאמַר אָמֵן
4. אָז יֹאמְרוּ בַגּוֹיִם: "הִגְדִּיל יְיָ לַעֲשׂוֹת עִם אֵלֶּה"
5. בָּרוּךְ שֶׁאָמַר וְהָיָה הָעוֹלָם, בָּרוּךְ הוּא

3

An Ethical Echo

Psalm 15 teaches us that telling the truth—אֱמֶת—is so important that only those who "speak truth in their hearts and have no slander on their tongues" will "live in God's house." The prophets, whose words we read in the haftarah, were also known as "prophets of truth," because they passed the truth of righteous and just behavior from God to the Jewish people.

Think About This!

It would be hard to find someone who's *never* told a lie! Maybe you ate a slice of the freshly baked apple pie meant for that night's dinner guests, and then pretended it wasn't you. Perhaps you forgot to walk the dog, but then claimed you did, so your dad wouldn't get upset. Or maybe you've joined in spreading false rumors about someone. What does the expression "to get caught in a web of lies" mean? In addition to being truthful to others, why do we need to be truthful to ourselves?

הַבּוֹחֵר בַּתּוֹרָה "the one who chooses the Torah"

הַבּוֹחֵר means "the one who chooses."

In this phrase, הַ is a prefix meaning "the one who."

בּוֹחֵר means _____.

הַבּוֹחֵר is built on the root בחר.

The root בחר tells us that "choose" is part of a word's meaning.

Below are lines from two prayers you have studied. Read each excerpt and circle all the words built on the root בחר. Then write the number of the line from each prayer next to the name of the prayer.

1. בָּרוּךְ אַתָּה, יְיָ אֱלֹהֵינוּ, מֶלֶךְ הָעוֹלָם, אֲשֶׁר בָּחַר־בָּנוּ מִכָּל־הָעַמִּים, וְנָתַן־לָנוּ אֶת־תּוֹרָתוֹ.
2. כִּי בָנוּ בָחַרְתָּ וְאוֹתָנוּ קִדַּשְׁתָּ מִכָּל הָעַמִּים

Kiddush _____

Blessing Before the Torah Reading _____

4

וּבְמֹשֶׁה עַבְדּוֹ "and Moses, God's servant"

וּבְמֹשֶׁה means "and Moses."

וּ is a prefix meaning _____.

מֹשֶׁה means _____.

עַבְדּוֹ means "God's servant."

עַבְדּוֹ is made up of two word-parts: עֶבֶד and the word ending וֹ ("his"). Because God is neither male nor female, we translate עַבְדּוֹ as "God's servant." In what ways was Moses God's servant?

_____

_____

When we are young, sometimes we are tempted to gossip or tell tales. As we mature, we begin to understand how hurtful such behavior can be.

וּבְיִשְׂרָאֵל עַמּוֹ "and Israel, God's people"

וּבְיִשְׂרָאֵל means "and Israel."

וּ means _____.

יִשְׂרָאֵל means _____.

עַמּוֹ means "God's people."

עַם means "people" or "nation."

וֹ at the end of a word means "his."

Because God is neither male nor female, we translate עַמּוֹ as "God's people."

"and prophets of truth and righteousness (justice)"

וּבִנְבִיאֵי means "and prophets of."

וּ means _____.

נְבִיאֵי means "prophets of."

הָאֱמֶת means "the truth."

הָ means _____.

אֱמֶת means _____.

Read the following prayer excerpts. Circle the word אֱמֶת in each line.

1. וְטַהֵר לִבֵּנוּ לְעָבְדְּךָ בֶּאֱמֶת

2. אֲשֶׁר נָתַן לָנוּ תּוֹרַת אֱמֶת וְחַיֵּי עוֹלָם נָטַע בְּתוֹכֵנוּ

3. אֱמֶת מַלְכֵּנוּ, אֶפֶס זוּלָתוֹ

4. תּוֹרַת אֱמֶת נָתַן לְעַמּוֹ אֵל עַל יַד נְבִיאוֹ נֶאֱמַן בֵּיתוֹ

5. הוֹלֵךְ תָּמִים וּפֹעֵל צֶדֶק וְדֹבֵר אֱמֶת בִּלְבָבוֹ

וָצֶדֶק means "and righteousness" or "and justice."

וָ means _____.

צֶדֶק means _____.

An Ethical Echo

The Hebrew word צְדָקָה comes from the word צֶדֶק ("righteousness" or "justice"). Giving tzedakah is a commandment and an obligation for all Jews. According to Jewish law, we should all give a portion of our earnings to those less fortunate. The highest level of tzedakah is when we give anonymously and so generously that a needy person can become self-sufficient.

Think About This!

What kinds of tzedakah—besides money—can we give? If you give food to a food bank or clothes to a clothing drive, is that tzedakah? Why? If you give a needy person a job, why is that considered the highest level of tzedakah? Do you think it is important to give tzedakah anonymously? Why or why not?

BLESSINGS AFTER THE HAFTARAH READING

When people you can count on—maybe your parent or your best friend—promise to do something, you usually rely on them because of your relationship and your trust. You believe your best friend's promise to keep it secret that you have a crush on that cute kid in math class. You believe your dad when he says he'll pick you up after the dance. Our tradition teaches us that the Jewish people have a relationship with God that is also built on trust, and that God watches over us, gives us life, and is merciful to us. We believe in God's promises.

We say four blessings after the haftarah reading. The first three blessings have to do with promises made by God to the Jewish people and our hope that those promises will come true.

The fourth and final blessing after the haftarah thanks God for the Torah, the worship service, the prophets, and Shabbat.

Practice reading the <u>first</u> of these blessings aloud.

1. בָּרוּךְ אַתָּה, יְיָ אֱלֹהֵינוּ, מֶלֶךְ הָעוֹלָם, צוּר כָּל הָעוֹלָמִים,

2. צַדִּיק בְּכָל הַדּוֹרוֹת, הָאֵל הַנֶּאֱמָן, הָאוֹמֵר וְעוֹשֶׂה,

3. הַמְדַבֵּר וּמְקַיֵּם, שֶׁכָּל־דְּבָרָיו אֱמֶת וָצֶדֶק.

4. נֶאֱמָן אַתָּה הוּא, יְיָ אֱלֹהֵינוּ, וְנֶאֱמָנִים דְּבָרֶיךָ, וְדָבָר אֶחָד

5. מִדְּבָרֶיךָ, אָחוֹר לֹא יָשׁוּב רֵיקָם, כִּי אֵל מֶלֶךְ נֶאֱמָן

6. וְרַחֲמָן אָתָּה.

7. בָּרוּךְ אַתָּה, יְיָ, הָאֵל הַנֶּאֱמָן בְּכָל־דְּבָרָיו.

Praised are You, Adonai our God, Ruler of the world, rock of all eternity,
righteous in all generations, the faithful God, the One who says and does,
the One who speaks and fulfills, for all God's words are truthful and just.

You are faithful, Adonai our God, and faithful are Your words, and not one of Your words
will return empty, for You are a faithful and compassionate God and Ruler.
Praised are You, Adonai, faithful in all Your words.

FLUENT READING

Practice reading blessings two, three, and four which are said after the הַפְטָרָה reading.

II

1. רַחֵם עַל־צִיּוֹן כִּי הִיא בֵּית חַיֵּינוּ, וְלַעֲלוּבַת נֶפֶשׁ תּוֹשִׁיעַ

2. בִּמְהֵרָה בְיָמֵינוּ. בָּרוּךְ אַתָּה, יְיָ, מְשַׂמֵּחַ צִיּוֹן בְּבָנֶיהָ.

III

3. שַׂמְּחֵנוּ, יְיָ אֱלֹהֵינוּ, בְּאֵלִיָּהוּ הַנָּבִיא עַבְדֶּךָ, וּבְמַלְכוּת בֵּית דָּוִד

4. מְשִׁיחֶךָ, בִּמְהֵרָה יָבֹא וְיָגֵל לִבֵּנוּ. עַל־כִּסְאוֹ לֹא־יֵשֶׁב זָר

5. וְלֹא־יִנְחֲלוּ עוֹד אֲחֵרִים אֶת־כְּבוֹדוֹ, כִּי בְשֵׁם קָדְשְׁךָ נִשְׁבַּעְתָּ

6. לּוֹ שֶׁלֹּא־יִכְבֶּה נֵרוֹ לְעוֹלָם וָעֶד. בָּרוּךְ אַתָּה, יְיָ, מָגֵן דָּוִד.

IV

7. עַל־הַתּוֹרָה, וְעַל־הָעֲבוֹדָה, וְעַל הַנְּבִיאִים, וְעַל־יוֹם הַשַּׁבָּת הַזֶּה,

8. שֶׁנָּתַתָּ־לָּנוּ, יְיָ אֱלֹהֵינוּ, לִקְדֻשָּׁה וְלִמְנוּחָה, לְכָבוֹד וּלְתִפְאָרֶת,

9. עַל־הַכֹּל, יְיָ אֱלֹהֵינוּ, אֲנַחְנוּ מוֹדִים לָךְ, וּמְבָרְכִים אוֹתָךְ.

10. יִתְבָּרַךְ שִׁמְךָ בְּפִי כָּל־חַי תָּמִיד לְעוֹלָם וָעֶד.

11. בָּרוּךְ אַתָּה, יְיָ, מְקַדֵּשׁ הַשַּׁבָּת.

ISBN 978-0-87441-766-1

9 780874 417661 >